IDENTIFICATION

IDENTIFICATION

ODYSSEYS

VALERIE BODDEN

CREATIVE EDUCATION · CREATIVE PAPERBACKS

Published by Creative Education and Creative Paperbacks
P.O. Box 227, Mankato, Minnesota 56002
Creative Education and Creative Paperbacks
are imprints of The Creative Company
www.thecreativecompany.us

Design by Blue Design (www.bluedes.com)
Production by Joe Kahnke
Art direction by Rita Marshall
Printed in China

Photographs by Alamy (The Advertising Archives, Cultura
Creative [RF], dpa picture alliance archive, epa european
pressphoto agency b.v., Keystone Pictures USA, Niday Picture
Library, Pablo Paul, Scenics & Science, Universal Images Group
North America LLC, A. T. Willett, ZUMA Press Inc.), Creative
Commons Wikimedia (Boston Public Library, CSIRO, Vic2015,
Zalman992), Flickr (The Littlejohn Collection/Sandor Teszler
Library/Wofford College, West Midlands Police), Getty Images
(Bloomberg, CBS Photo Archive, Stegerphoto), iStockphoto
(Darren Mower), Michigan State Police, Shutterstock (Africa
Studio, Coprid, Henrik Larsson, seeyou)

Library of Congress Cataloging-in-Publication Data
Names: Bodden, Valerie, author.
Title: Identification / Valerie Bodden.
Series: Odysseys in crime scene science.
Includes bibliographical references and index.
Summary: An in-depth look at how crime scene investigators
use evidence found at crime scenes to identify victims
and suspects, employing real-life examples such as The
Nightstalker case.
Identifiers: LCCN 2015027739 / ISBN 978-1-60818-681-5
(hardcover) / ISBN 978-1-62832-470-9 (pbk) / ISBN 978-1-
56660-717-9 (eBook)
Subjects: LCSH: 1. Evidence, Criminal—Juvenile literature.
2. Criminal investigation—Juvenile literature. 3. Criminals—
Identification—Juvenile literature. 4. Forensic sciences—
Juvenile literature.
Classification: LCC HV8073.8.B626 2016 / DDC 363.25/8—dc23

CCSS: RI 8.1, 2, 3, 4, 5, 8, 10; RI 9-10.1, 2, 3, 4, 5, 8, 10; RI 11-12.1,
2, 3, 4, 5, 10; RST 6-8.1, 2, 5, 6, 10; RST 9-10.1, 2, 5, 6, 10; RST
11-12.1, 2, 5, 6, 10

First Edition HC 9 8 7 6 5 4 3 2 1
First Edition PBK 9 8 7 6 5 4 3 2 1

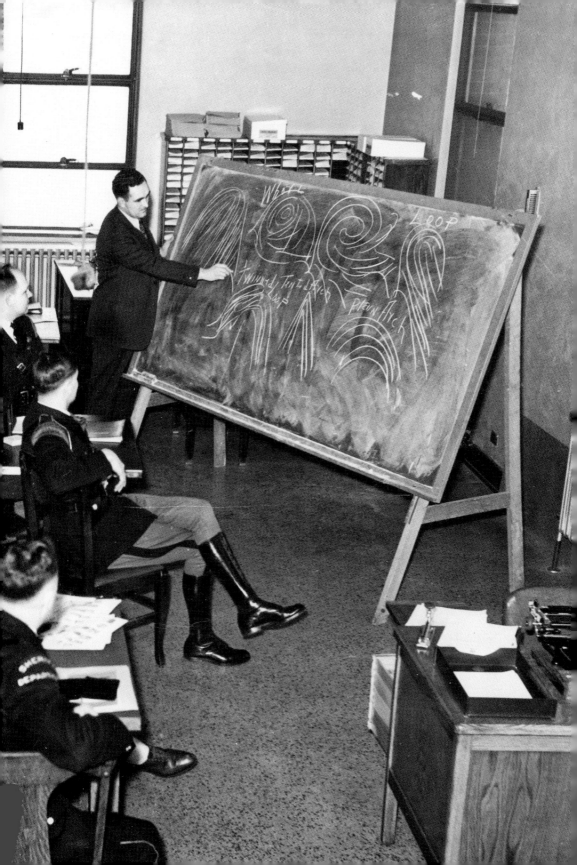

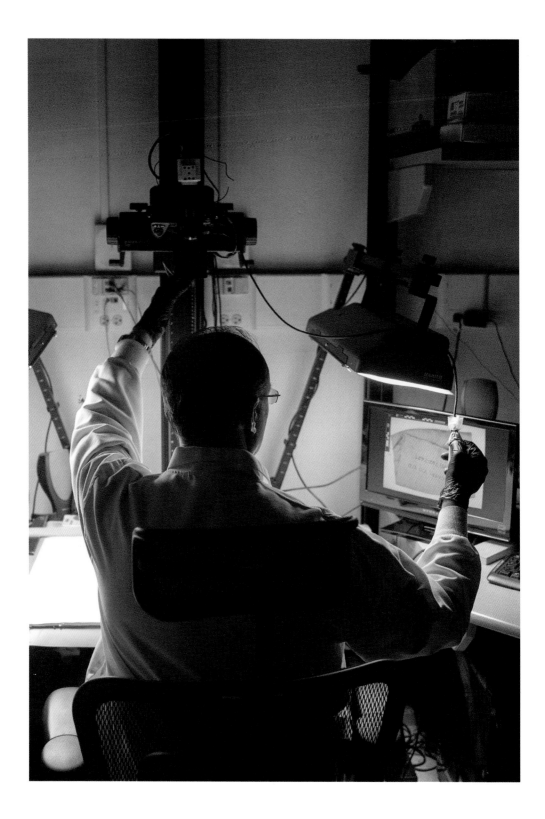

CONTENTS

Introduction

Blue and red lights sweep across the front of a home. They reflect off jagged shards of glass in a broken first-floor window. Inside, books and pictures have been tossed to the floor. Papers hang from ransacked drawers. Two plates—their food still warm—sit on the kitchen table. A small red spot stains the floor under one of the chairs. This looks like a crime scene. But by the time police

OPPOSITE: The first police officer to arrive at a crime scene secures the area with crime scene tape and other barriers so that no unauthorized persons enter or leave the crime scene before it has been processed. A logbook is used to keep track of who enters the crime scene.

arrived, the house was empty. Now investigators must use crime scene science to help solve the mystery of what happened here—and who did it.

Crime scene science is also referred to as forensic science. Forensic science is simply science that is used to solve crimes and provide facts in a legal trial. Solving a crime often involves many forensic scientists, each specializing in a different area. Many of those forensic scientists are involved in identifying suspects, victims, and weapons found at the crime scene. Some analyze fingerprints and DNA. Others examine bullets and guns. Some compare hairs and fibers found at the scene. The results of this critical step in an investigation can help bring criminals to justice.

Uncovering What's Hidden

Forensic science is based on Locard's exchange principle, which forensic scientists sum up as, "Every contact leaves a trace." The principle is named for the French forensic scientist Edmond Locard, who developed it. It means that people cannot enter a scene without leaving evidence of their presence. And they can't leave without taking some part of the scene with them. When you enter a room, for example, you might touch something and leave a fingerprint. Or you might leave behind a hair or a piece of fiber from your clothing. Your shoes might pick up fibers from the carpet or a piece of fur from the dog.

The first step in any crime scene investigation is to look for all these traces of contact. This step is carried out by crime scene investigators (CSIs). They are trained to collect fingerprints, blood, bullet casings, hair, fibers, and any other evidence that might help solve the case.

But this evidence means little on its own. It needs to be analyzed and interpreted to determine its origin.

That is why the CSIs package all the evidence they've found and send it to crime labs. There, forensic scientists specializing in fingerprint, DNA, ballistics, document, and trace evidence analysis examine the evidence. For some tests, they use basic instruments such as magnifying glasses and microscopes. For others, they use specialized instruments such as spectrometers. Identifying a substance might also involve complex chemical reactions that break substances down into their base parts.

The goals of this analysis are to identify victims and suspects and to establish a connection between suspects and the crime scene. Different types of evidence provide different degrees of certainty in the identification process. Some types of evidence can be shown to come from only one individual. Every person's fingerprints are unique, for example. And, aside from identical twins, no two people have the same DNA.

ut fingerprint and DNA evidence aren't always available. Criminals might wear gloves, making it impossible for investigators to find fingerprints. And even if there are fingerprints, they might be smudged. Or there may be only a partial print. In addition, experts estimate that they find DNA evidence in only about 10 percent of cases.

WANTED

JOHN DILLINGER, with alias,

FRANK SULLIVAN

Photograph tak

DESCRIPTION

Age, 31 years
Height, 5 feet 7-1/8 inches
Weight, 153 pounds
Build, medium
Hair, medium chestnut
Eyes, grey
Complexion, medium
Occupation, machinist
Marks and scars, 1/2 inch scar
    back left hand; scar middle
    upper lip; brown mole between
    eyebrows
Mustache

ACT

Permanent Prints

Fingerprints begin forming in the womb at five months. They remain the same throughout a person's life. Even if the skin of the finger is damaged, it will grow back in the same ridge pattern. (Serious scars may interrupt the pattern, but the print will still be unique.) Even so, some criminals have tried to hide their identity by purposely damaging their fingerprints. Noted early-1900s gangster John Dillinger dipped his hands in acid to burn off his fingerprints. But after a while, the ridges reappeared. Gangster Robert Phillips went even farther. He had his fingertips surgically removed and replaced with skin from his chest. What he didn't account for was that ridge patterns below the top knuckle are also unique. Authorities used these patterns to identify him.

January 25, 1934

CRIMINAL RECORD

As John Dillinger, #14395, received State Reformatory, Pendleton, Indiana, September 16, 1924; crime, assault and battery with intent to rob and conspiracy to commit a felony; sentences, 2 to 14 years and 10 to 20 years respectively;

As John Dillinger, #13225, received State Prison, Michigan City, Indiana, July 16, 1929; transferred from Indiana State Reformatory; paroled under Reformatory jurisdiction, May 10, 1933; parole revoked by Governor – considered as delinquent parolee;

As John Dillinger, #10587, arrested Police Department, Dayton, Ohio, September 22, 1933; charge, fugitive; turned over to Allen County, Ohio, authorities;

Most of the evidence found at crime scenes is class evidence. This type of evidence cannot be linked to only one possible source. But it can be sorted, or classified, as belonging to a group of items with the same properties. Hair and fibers are common types of class evidence. Say a red fiber is found at a crime scene. Then investigators find a red shirt at the suspect's house. Analysis shows that the shirt is made from the same kind of material as the fiber found at the scene. The same dye was used on both as well. This does not necessarily mean that the fiber came from this shirt. Anyone who owned this same kind of shirt could have also left this kind of fiber behind. The most investigators can say based on the fiber evidence is that the suspect cannot be ruled out.

Even though it can't be individualized, class evi-

Investigators use high-powered microscopes to note any differences in hairs and fibers. Here, a microscope reveals the difference in the thickness and texture of two human hairs.

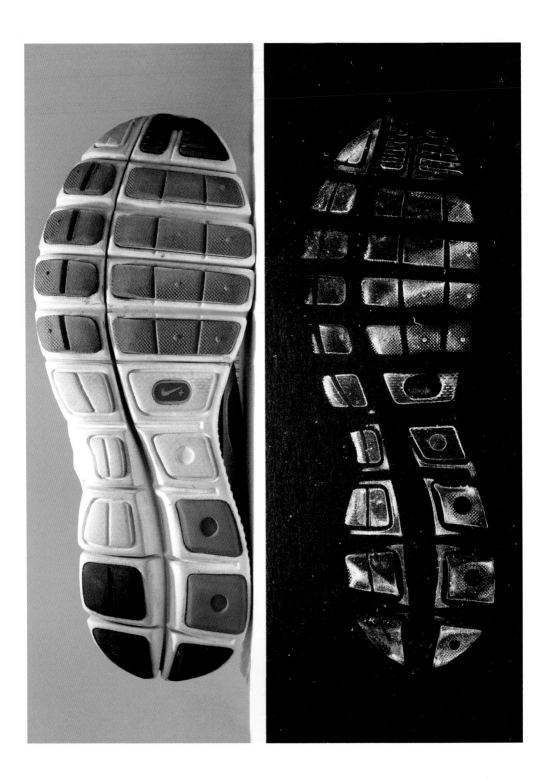

dence is still useful. It may be so unique that it points to a particular suspect. For example, in a case in Florida, investigators found a bloody shoe print in a murder victim's house. The print showed a hole in the sole of the shoe. When investigators tested the suspect's shoe, it had a hole in the same place. Of course, many people may have owned the same kind of shoes. But it was unlikely that any of them had a hole in exactly the same place and of exactly the same size.

Class evidence is also useful in connecting a suspect with the crime scene. The more pieces of evidence that connect a suspect to the crime, the more convincing the case against him will be. For example, in 2000, the body of a young girl was found in West Sussex, England. Police suspected a local man named Roy Whiting. But they needed evidence to connect him to the crime. The girl's shoe had fibers from a sweatshirt on it. A search of Whiting's car gave police a sweatshirt made from the same kind of fiber. That shirt had a hair on it that was similar to the victim's hair. Fibers found on the victim were also consistent with fibers from Whiting's socks, other clothing, and van. Because there was no DNA evidence, the defense held that Whiting could not be proved guilty. But the prosecution argued that so many consistencies between the evidence and Whiting added up to a unique profile. Whiting was sentenced to life in prison.

As they work with evidence, forensic scientists have to be careful not to **contaminate** it. DNA analysts need to wear gloves, lab coats, face masks, and hairnets. Otherwise, they could pass their own DNA to the sample. They must also use new disposable tools for each test. In one case, a man was arrested based on DNA evidence.

But the man's phone records showed he was 280 miles (450 km) away at the time of the crime. Investigators later discovered that analysts at the lab had reused tools that had previously been used on tests of the man's DNA in a separate incident.

Forensic scientists have to document every step of their process. Such documentation must show the chain of custody for the evidence. This is a record of who had the evidence, when they had it, and what they did with it. Any testing done on the evidence, along with the results, is also recorded. This helps to show that the evidence was not tampered with. If these procedures are not followed, the evidence may not be **admissible** in court. Because forensic evidence will eventually help determine whether a suspect is convicted or cleared, it must meet the highest quality standards.

Uniquely Yours

For more than 100 years, police departments have used fingerprints to identify criminals and victims. Everyone—even identical twins—has unique fingerprints. So these marks are among the most valuable evidence at any crime scene. Fingerprints are formed by the raised lines—called friction ridges—on the tips of the fingers. Traces of sweat, oils, and dirt collect on the ridges. When you touch something, these substances get

OPPOSITE: For decades, police departments and investigators around the world have been using special powders to reveal fingerprints that are otherwise invisible. Once these prints are revealed, they are photographed and then carefully lifted with clear tape.

transferred to that object in the shape of the friction ridges.

Each individual's friction ridges form a unique pattern. But those patterns can be grouped into three general categories. Loops enter the finger from one side, curve around, and exit the finger on the same side. Whorls form circles or spirals. Arches make a rainbow shape as they travel from one side of the finger to the other.

A fingerprint from a crime scene is referred to as an unknown print because its source is not known. A fingerprint from a suspect is called a known

About 65 percent of all fingerprints in the world have loop patterns. Another 30 percent have whorls. Only 5 percent have arches. Each of your fingers has a different fingerprint pattern.

print. A fingerprint examiner compares the known and unknown prints to determine if they match. Such comparisons can be made using a small magnifier called a loupe. The examiner looks for minutiae, or places where the ridges make irregular changes. They might split into a Y-shape or suddenly end, for example. Or they might cross other ridges. In the United States, examiners must find 12 minutiae in common to declare a match. Finding even a single difference between the prints means there is no match.

Sometimes fingerprints are found at the crime scene before police have identified a suspect. In these cases, the fingerprints can be uploaded into local, state, or national databases. The Next Generation Identification (NGI) system is a national database maintained by the Federal Bureau of Investigation (FBI). It stores the fingerprints

A fingerprint examiner compares the known and unknown prints.... even a single difference between the prints means there is no match.

of known criminals, as well as unknown fingerprints from crime scenes. The system searches for matches between a crime scene print and those in the database. The closest matches are returned—usually within half an hour. The fingerprint examiner can then review the results to determine if any of the prints are an exact match. The NGI, which replaced the FBI's former fingerprint database in 2014, also stores palm prints. These are as unique as fingerprints and are found even more often at crime scenes.

Fingerprints were essential in solving the case of The Nightstalker. This nickname referred to a man who

roamed Los Angeles in the early 1980s. He killed men and attacked women. A fingerprint from the suspect's car was uploaded into the city's brand-new fingerprint database. It returned a match: Richard Ramirez. He was sentenced to death.

While fingerprinting is an old technique in crime scene science, DNA analysis is among the newest. DNA stands for deoxyribonucleic acid. It carries the **genetic** code that makes each of us unique. As author David Fisher puts

You Be the Scientist

Ask your friends or family to help you practice your forensic skills. First, have five people make an ink fingerprint. Each person's fingerprint should be on a separate paper labeled with his or her name. Then leave the room. While you are gone, each person should make another ink fingerprint on a different surface, such as a cardboard box or a candy wrapper. When they are done, they should leave the items in a pile so you can't see who used which surface. Try to match the fingerprint papers with the fingerprints on the objects. You may need to use a magnifying glass. Look for loops, whorls, and arches as well as places where the ridges stop or branch. How many of the fingerprints did you correctly identify?

it, "DNA is the biological equivalent of fingerprints." In fact, using DNA for forensic purposes is often referred to as DNA fingerprinting. It can also be called DNA testing, typing, or profiling.

NA is carried in the nucleus of each of your body's cells (except red blood cells, which have no nucleus). At crime scenes, DNA is usually found in body fluids such as blood, saliva, semen, urine, and even sweat. But it can also be found in hair roots or skin cells. These substances might be found on cups, cigarette butts,

envelopes, gum, or any other items a suspect has come into contact with.

DNA is extracted from cells using chemicals and enzymes that separate the DNA from other cell parts. The DNA can then be copied through a process known as polymerase chain reaction (PCR). In this process, an enzyme called polymerase is added to the extracted DNA. The mixture is then heated and cooled in a series of cycles. This stimulates the polymerase to create new copies of the DNA. The process can create millions or even billions of copies of the DNA. This means that a tiny DNA sample can provide enough material for testing. Even a single hair or a bloodstain smaller than the period at the end of this sentence is often enough.

DNA analysts focus on specific regions (or loci) of DNA that contain short, repeating patterns called short

Scientists sometimes test mosquitoes, fleas, and cockroaches found at a crime scene. If the insects have consumed blood that matches a suspect's DNA, it can prove he was at the scene.

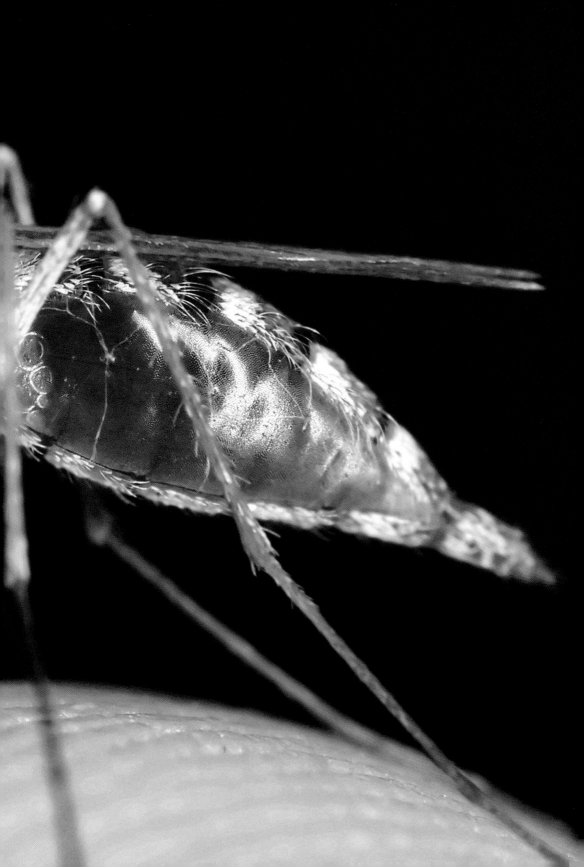

tandem repeats (STRs). By analyzing the STRs at 13 loci, analysts can create a unique DNA profile. "It's the combination of those different locations that makes the DNA profile a powerful identifier," says Douglas Hares, who oversees the FBI's DNA database. "It's like a license plate. If you only search three letters or numbers of a license plate, you will get a lot of false matches. We require the threshold to be much higher to prevent those false matches."

The profile for DNA found at a crime scene can be compared with the DNA profile of a suspect. (A suspect's DNA is usually obtained by swabbing the cheek or drawing blood.) If the profiles do not match at any 1 of the 13 areas tested, the suspect cannot be the source of the DNA. A match is declared only if all 13 loci match. If there is no suspect, the DNA profile from the crime scene can be uploaded into the FBI's Combined DNA Index System (CODIS). This database contains DNA profiles of convicted offenders as well as unknown DNA profiles from crime scenes. CODIS searches for matches in the system and returns results to the lab.

When DNA from cell nuclei is not available, scientists can sometimes use another form of DNA, called **mitochondrial** DNA (mtDNA). Because mtDNA is passed on only from the mother, everyone has the same mtDNA as his or her mother. So mtDNA can be used to determine that a person belongs to a particular family line. But it cannot be used to identify a specific individual. One advantage to using mtDNA is that each mitochondrion contains thousands of copies of mtDNA. Because there are so many copies, mtDNA can often be found in sources in which the nuclear DNA has been degraded.

Connecting the Dots

Many forms of evidence can show a connection between a suspect and the crime scene. If a crime involves the use of a gun, one of the most important aspects of the investigation will be ballistics. The inside of rifle and handgun barrels consists of a series of spiral grooves. The raised areas between the grooves are known as lands. As a bullet travels down the barrel, these lands and grooves leave

OPPOSITE: Because they depend on expert interpretation to determine a match, the reliability of ballistics tests (among other such forensic tests) has recently been called into question. There is no scientific data to support the accuracy of these tests.

an impression on it. The number, direction of spiral, and width of lands and grooves vary from one weapon to another. These marks can be used to identify the manufacturer, make, and model of the gun that fired the bullets.

Sometimes firearms examiners can go even farther. They might be able to pinpoint the specific gun that shot the bullets. When a firearm is made, the tool that creates the grooves in the barrel also leaves tiny imperfections, known as striations. Like lands and grooves, the striations

Ballistics analysis of the ammunition that killed Confederate General Stonewall Jackson showed it was a .67-caliber ball. This ammunition was used by Confederate, not Union, troops.

are imprinted on the bullet when the gun is fired.

To determine if a bullet came from a specific gun, the firearms examiner first fires a test bullet from the gun. It is usually fired into a water tank so the bullet will not be damaged. The examiner then compares the test bullet with the crime scene bullet using a comparison microscope. This device consists of two microscopes connected together. It shows the two bullets side-by-side. Both are magnified the same amount. The bullets must have identical striation patterns to be considered a match.

Sometimes, instead of lines on bullets, scientists have to analyze written lines on paper. This is the job of questioned document examiners. In their analysis, questioned document examiners consider the paper and ink with which a document was written. Using a spectrometer, they can identify the dyes in the ink. They can also use

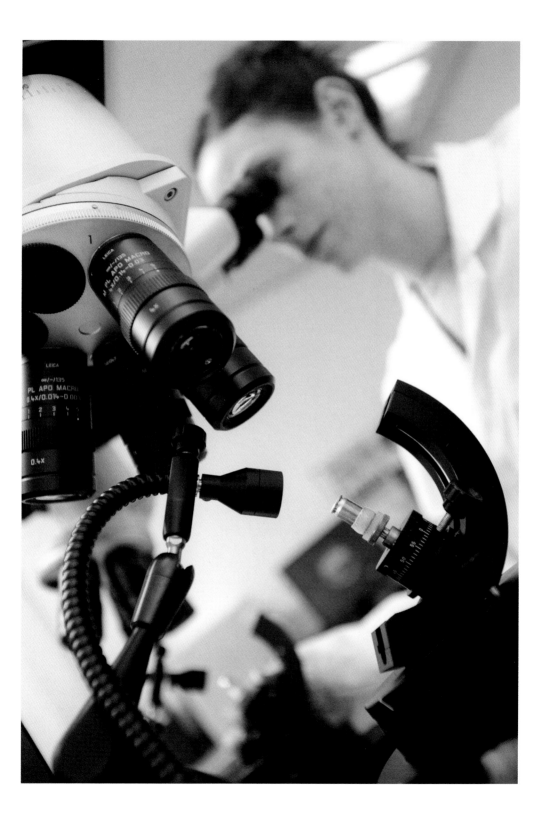

chemical reactions to figure out the substances that make up the ink and paper. In 1981, a forger attempted to sell the supposed diaries of German dictator Adolf Hitler. Testing revealed that the ink used in the diaries had not existed when the diaries were said to have been written. And the paper contained a whitening agent that hadn't been introduced until after Hitler's 1945 death.

In addition to analyzing what the document is made of, examiners look at the handwriting within it. Unique features of a person's handwriting tend to show up in everything he writes. For example, a person may dot an *i* or cross a *t* the same way every time. The slant of a person's writing also tends to remain constant. So does the relative size of their letters. By looking at a sample under a microscope, handwriting examiners can also tell whether a person's writing was shaky. They can spot places where the pen was lifted. These are often signs of trying to copy another person's writing or to disguise their own. In some cases, **linguists** are also called in to analyze a document. They look for similarities in word choice and phrasing between documents. These might indicate that the documents were written by the same person.

Sometimes evidence comes not from the hands but from the feet. Foot impressions can be examined to determine the brand of shoes a suspect was wearing. Details such

as wear marks can help set a suspect's shoe print apart from others who wear the same brand. They might even help investigators tell if the person walks with a limp or was carrying a heavy object. If the suspect has bitten the victim, the bite marks left behind might also be used as evidence. A forensic odontologist (dentist) can compare the bite marks at the scene to the suspect's teeth.

Much of the evidence at a crime scene is so small it would be easy to overlook. But sometimes these items, known as trace evidence, are the key to solving a case. Hair found at a crime scene can be compared with hair from the victim or a suspect. Analysts look at features such as hair color, width, length, and curl. They also look at microscopic characteristics. If the questioned hair differs from the known hair, the individual can be ruled out as the source of the questioned hair. Hair cannot be

Cold Cases

Both fingerprints and DNA have been used to solve many old, unsolved cases, often referred to as cold cases. In 2008, police officers in Nebraska uploaded fingerprints from a 1978 murder into the national fingerprint database. Within five hours, they had identified the killer in the 30-year-old case. In many cold cases, evidence was not submitted for DNA analysis during the original investigation. (It may have been collected before the capabilities for such analysis existed.) But this evidence can now be tested. In one cold case, the killer had strangled a victim with a phone cord. The cord had been saved and was tested for DNA. The result was successfully matched to a suspect. And it even helped to identify him as the offender in another, similar murder.

definitively matched to a specific individual through comparison alone. But if the root is still attached, the hair can be sent for DNA analysis. If there is no root, it can still provide mtDNA.

ibers can also be an important source of trace evidence. Analysts can determine the type of fiber by checking its refractive index. This is a measure of how much it makes light bend. Chemical tests can also help determine the fiber type. Analysts can figure out the exact color of a fiber using a microspectrophotometer. This device mea-

sures how the fiber reflects and absorbs light. It creates a "fingerprint" of the color. In cases where the dye is difficult to identify, it may be put through chemical analysis. This can separate out the different chemicals used to make the dye.

I n crimes involving vehicles or forced entry into a building, paint chips and glass are often found. Paint chips are generally made up of many layers. These layers can be examined under a microscope with polarized light. Additionally, a scanning electron microscope uses electrons to identify the elements in each layer. In some cases, the chemicals making up paint layers are heated until they break down into identifiable gases. To test glass, analysts examine its refractive index and density. Sometimes, a glass or paint chip can be fitted into the object it came from, almost like a puzzle piece. In these cases, the evidence is considered an exact match. Otherwise, glass and paint chips are class evidence.

Scientists can also examine traces of soil to discover if they are similar to the soil at a crime scene. They look for the presence of minerals, dead leaves, and moisture content. Pollen grains found in the soil can indicate the presence of plants that grow only in specific areas.

"Geek Chic"

Almost since the time forensic science was developed, fictional characters have been using it to solve crimes. Perhaps the most famous fictional detective is Sherlock Holmes, created by Scottish author Sir Arthur Conan Doyle in the 1880s. Doyle had his star detective using forensic science even before it was put into wide practice by real-life investigators. In the course of his stories, Holmes often relies on fingerprint, footprint, and document

OPPOSITE: Between 1886 and 1928, Sir Arthur Conan Doyle wrote 4 novels and 56 short stories featuring Sherlock Holmes. The character was based on one of Doyle's medical school professors, doctor Joseph Bell, who was known for his keen observations and intelligence.

analysis to identify the culprit.

Today, forensics fiction is more popular than ever. The television drama *CSI: Crime Scene Investigation* debuted on CBS in 2000. By the time it went off the air in 2015, it had a worldwide viewership of more than 60 million people. Other crime dramas featuring forensic scientists soon hit the air as well. Among them are *Bones*, *NCIS*, *Cold Case*, and *Without a Trace*.

As a result of such shows, public interest in forensic science has grown rapidly. According to media professor Robert Thompson, "It's 'geek chic,' the idea that kids who excel in science and math can grow up to be cool. This is long overdue.... Cops and cowboys and doctors and lawyers have been done to death."

In many cases, the portrayal of forensic science on TV is much different from how it works in real life. For

Much of the technology shown on TV is so advanced—and expensive—that it is used in only a few labs around the world.

example, on *CSI*, the same characters who investigate crime scenes also analyze the evidence in the lab. In reality, those would be completely separate jobs. In addition, much of the technology shown on TV is so advanced—and expensive—that it is used in only a few labs around the world. Or, it might not exist at all. "They do a gas chromatograph, and the suspect's driver's license pops up. That's just not possible," said Dan Royse, a special agent with the Tennessee Bureau of Investigation.

In addition, the pace of forensic analysis is much faster on TV than in reality. Characters on a television drama can investigate a crime, analyze the evidence, and

Factual Fiction

Novelist Jeffery Deaver's works about quadriplegic detective Lincoln Rhyme rely heavily on accurate forensic science. In *The Devil's Teardrop* (1999), Rhyme uses real-life techniques to analyze the handwriting in a document. "I noticed there was a tremble in his handwriting. That's what happens when somebody tries to disguise their writing.... I checked the lowercase *i* in 'two miles' and the dot was a devil's teardrop. That confirmed it." Deaver says that it is often the most realistic parts of his novels that readers question. "Some of Lincoln Rhyme's deductions, readers say 'nobody can do this—one fiber, you make this deduction with one fiber, that's absurd.' That's accurate, and that's the parts of the books that they think are unbelievable," he said.

arrest the bad guy in 60 minutes. But real-life forensic examinations often take months. DNA labs generally try to analyze and report on a DNA sample within 30 days. But this standard is often not met because of massive backlogs of evidence. Other forensic examinations take time, too. "I think our system has been hampered by shows like *CSI*, which show people doing things they cannot do, or doing them at a speed that's impossible," said Dr. Herbert Leon MacDonell, director of a forensics lab in New York. "I don't care how long you've worked matching bullets, when you have a bullet, you put it under the microscope, you compare it to the evidence bullet—it's going to take a while. You don't sit down and say, 'Yup, chief, it's a match.'"

Of course, the creators of *CSI* and other television shows aren't trying to make their shows 100 percent accurate. As *CSI* creator Anthony Zuiker said, "Our job really is to make great television, first and foremost.... I think Americans know that DNA doesn't come back in 20 minutes. I think Americans know that there's not some magical computer that you press and the guy's face pops up and where he lives. [I] think America knows that the time sheets when you're doing one hour of television have to be fudged a bit."

ut some people in the legal community aren't so sure that all Americans know the difference between fact

and fiction when it comes to what they see on TV. They especially worry about how such shows might influence jurors in real-life cases. Since 2002, debate has raged over whether crime shows cause a phenomenon known as the "*CSI* Effect," leading jurors to have unrealistic expectations based on what they have seen on TV. Both prosecutors and defense attorneys have claimed that the *CSI* Effect negatively impacts their cases.

Prosecutors say that shows like *CSI* have led jurors to believe that there must be DNA and other scientific evidence in every case. They demand this evidence even when eyewitness evidence clearly points to the suspect. Sometimes they expect it even after the suspect has confessed. In a 2008 poll, 22 percent of jurors said they expected to see DNA evidence in every criminal trial. Crime shows "create too much of an expectation," said sergeant Connie Justice of the Memphis Police Department. "[Viewers] think we can get DNA off of every single object, that there are full staffs analyzing it, and that we can get a single answer. If we don't get every type of answer, it's like we've done something wrong. It's a tough act to follow." When jurors are given less evidence than they see on TV, prosecutors say, they may be more likely to acquit the defendant. To counteract this effect, some prosecutors have begun to bring in expert witnesses to testify about why there might not be DNA evidence at the scene. They also talk about why such evidence isn't needed for a conviction. Prosecutors are also having more evidence tested than necessary, which adds to expense, as well as lab backlogs.

Defense attorneys, on the other hand, claim that the *CSI* Effect negatively impacts their case. It might lead jurors to think that scientific evidence is always right. "If anything, *CSI*'s pro-police, pro-forensics story exalts forensics evidence, ... bolstering it along with the prosecution's case," according to media law professor Kimberlianne Podlas. As a result, jurors might see forensic evidence as more important to the case than it actually is. This might lead them to discount other, more important, evidence. Or they may believe the forensic evidence allows stronger conclusions to be drawn than it does. For example, they might think fiber comparison can provide an exact match to a suspect.

Others in the legal community argue that there is no such thing as the *CSI* Effect, except in lawyers' imaginations. They point out that shows like *CSI* rarely venture into the courtroom, so they shouldn't impact what happens at a trial.

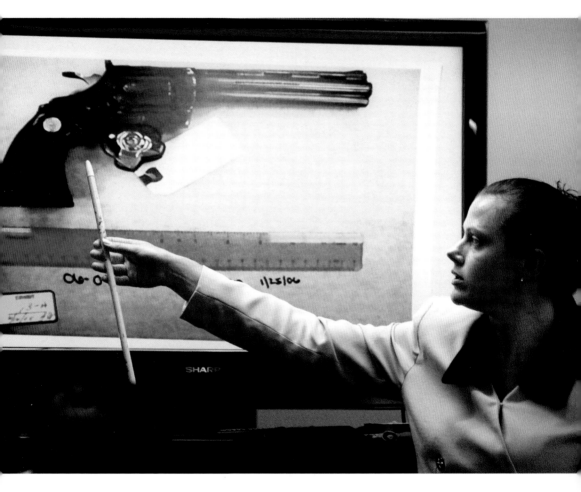

Fixing Forensics

One other result of the *CSI* Effect
is the explosion of forensic science
as a career choice. Hundreds of
colleges across the U.S. now offer
forensic science programs. Some
provide degrees in specific fields
such as forensic DNA. A degree
in biology, chemistry, or a related
field can also prepare a student for
a career in forensic science. Many
forensic scientists are civilians. But
some police officers hold these

positions as well. Forensic scientists may work at state or local crime labs or at private labs. Most positions require an internship or extensive on-the-job training.

orensic scientists need good communication skills. Once they have finished testing the evidence in a case, they must send a report of the results to the lead detective. If a suspect has not already been identified, the report may help police zero in on a subject. If a suspect has already been arrested, the results may help the prosecutor make a strong case. Or they may prove the suspect's innocence. If

the case goes to trial, the forensic scientist may be called to testify regarding the testing they performed.

Several issues regarding the use of forensic testing for identification have been raised in recent years. For example, crime labs in many states have been criticized for mishandling DNA evidence, leading to contamination. Backlogs have become another huge issue, especially when it comes to DNA testing. According to the National Institute of Justice (NIJ), a backlogged case is one that has not been completed within 30 days of being received by the crime lab. The NIJ estimates that more than 100,000 DNA cases are backlogged nationwide.

Another issue sometimes faced by lab workers is a bias in favor of prosecution. In some cases, police officers tell scientists the circumstances of the crime. Knowing whom the police suspect may bias the scientist against him or her. In addition, many crime labs are government agencies. As a result, they are often seen as part of the prosecution's "team." They may feel pressured by the rest of the "team" to provide evidence against a suspect. Even private crime labs may want to give prosecutors the desired results to ensure continued business.

ome people also question how scientific many aspects of forensic science really are. In 2009, the National Academy of Sciences (NAS) issued a report on the state of forensic science. It said that apart from DNA analysis,

Sacco and Vanzetti

On April 15, 1920, two security guards in Massachusetts were robbed and killed. Eyewitness testimony led officers to Bartolomeo Vanzetti and Nicola Sacco. The suspects were found carrying guns. Sacco also had bullets made by the same company as those found at the crime scene. Ballistics testing showed that Sacco's pistol had fired one of the fatal bullets. The men were sentenced to death. But then a man claiming to be an expert said the ballistics evidence was wrong. The sentence was delayed. In 1927, the Bureau of Forensic Ballistics in New York matched Sacco's gun to the bullet from the crime scene. Sacco and Vanzetti were executed later that year. New tests in 1961 and 1983 confirmed the results of the original ballistics test. Even so, rumors that the men were innocent persist.

no forensic method had been shown to consistently and accurately connect evidence with a specific individual. A large part of the problem, according to many critics, is that most forensic disciplines were developed by the law enforcement community rather than by scientists. As a result, they have never been put through rigorous scientific testing. (The exception is DNA testing, which was first developed for biological research.) "You can't take a few case studies and say, 'Oh, it worked on these people; it must be reliable,'" said Karen Kafadar, who was part of the NAS committee that wrote the report.

Among the forensic sciences most called into question have been hair, fiber, and bite mark analysis. Ballistics, handwriting, and footprint analysis have also been criticized. All of these fields rely on expert interpretation to determine a match. In most cases, there is no scientific data to support how accurate such matches are.

Even fingerprints, once considered foolproof, have faced questions. In April 2004, police mistakenly identified a fingerprint at the scene of a Spanish train bombing in Madrid as belonging to an Oregon man. The real perpetrator was later identified as a man from Algeria. The NAS said that this case should "surely signal caution against simple ... assumptions about the reliability of fingerprint evidence." Some scientists estimate that as many as 1 out of every 100 crime scene fingerprints could be misidentified. Others counter that no significant problems in accuracy have been found throughout the long history of fingerprint analysis.

Those performing the tests can still make mistakes, though. Forensic scientists' mistakes can have serious consequences, including wrongful convictions. Fortunate-

Since 1989, the Innocence Project has used DNA to clear more than 340 wrongly convicted individuals.

ly, forensic science can also help correct those mistakes. Since 1989, the Innocence Project has used DNA to clear more than 340 wrongly convicted individuals. The organization reports that in nearly half of those cases, improper or unvalidated forensic science played a role in the conviction. For example, in 1989, Steven Barnes was convicted of murder. The conviction was based on hairs found in his pickup truck that an expert said were similar to the victim's hair. The expert also said that soil samples from the truck were similar to soil at the crime scene. After Barnes spent nearly 20 years in prison, DNA testing proved him innocent, and he was released.

As a result of such wrongful convictions, the NAS recommended a number of improvements. One of the

00052pr001.931230.tiff

most important was making crime labs independent of law enforcement. The NAS also said that forensic labs should be subjected to stricter quality control standards. In addition, the organization called for scientific research to confirm the reliability of various forensic disciplines.

Along with these improvements, the future of forensic science is likely to bring with it new technology to help with the identification process. For example, companies are beginning to develop portable DNA tests that can provide instant DNA analysis at a crime scene. Within the lab, more of the DNA testing process will likely be automated. Researchers have also begun exploring how to create a computer-generated image of a suspect based on the hair, eye, and skin color revealed in DNA. Aside from DNA, researchers are also exploring new identification methods such as facial recognition, iris scans, and voiceprints. Some are even looking for ways to analyze the chemicals in an individual's sweat.

As old forensics methods are evaluated and new ones are adopted, the investigation of crimes will continue to hinge on identification. Investigators will always need ways to determine the identity of both victims and suspects. And they will need ways to connect those suspects to the crime scene. For that, they will continue to rely on extreme crime scene science.

Glossary

admissible   allowed to be used in a legal trial

ballistics   the study of firearms and the firing of ammunition

contaminate   to introduce foreign material

density   a measurement indicating how much mass an object has compared to its volume

DNA   abbreviation for deoxyribonucleic acid, a substance found in the cells that contains genetic information that determines a person's characteristics, such as eye color

electron   a minuscule, negatively charged particle that travels around the nucleus of an atom

enzymes   proteins that can start or speed up a chemical reaction

gas chromatograph   an instrument used to separate a sample into its component gases

genetic   having to do with genes, which transfer traits from a parent to a child

impression   a mark made by pressing one object into another

linguists   people who study language

mitochondrial   related to structures in cells that convert food to usable energy

nucleus	the part of the cell that contains DNA and controls cell growth
polarized light	light that vibrates in a single plane
quadriplegic	a person who is paralyzed from the neck down
spectrometers	instruments that identify substances by measuring how they absorb, reflect, or transmit light
trace evidence	tiny pieces of evidence, often too small to be seen by the naked eye, that can serve to identify an individual or connect the individual to a specific location

Selected Bibliography

Committee on Identifying the Needs of the Forensic Sciences Community, National Research Council. *Strengthening Forensic Science in the United States: A Path Forward.* Washington, D.C.: National Academies Press, 2009. https://www.ncjrs.gov/pdffiles1/nij/grants/228091.pdf.

Dale, W. Mark, and Wendy S. Becker. *The Crime Scene: How Forensic Science Works.* New York: Kaplan, 2007.

Fisher, Barry A. J. *Techniques of Crime Scene Investigation.* 7th ed. Boca Raton, Fla.: CRC Press, 2004.

Genge, N. E. *The Forensic Casebook: The Science of Crime Scene Investigation.* New York: Ballantine, 2002.

Houck, Max M. *Forensic Science: Modern Methods of Solving Crime.* Westport, Conn.: Praeger, 2007.

National Forensic Science Technology Center. *A Simplified Guide to Forensic Science.* http://www.forensicsciencesimplified .org/index.htm.

Owen, David. *Hidden Evidence: 50 True Crimes and How Forensic Science Helped Solve Them.* 2nd ed. Buffalo, N.Y.: Firefly Books, 2009.

Ricciuti, Edward. *Science 101: Forensics.* New York: HarperCollins, 2007.

Websites

FBI: Fun & Games
http://www.fbi.gov/fun-games

Check out the tools FBI agents use, and learn how the FBI analyzes evidence.

PBS NOVA: Extract Your Own DNA
http://www.pbs.org/wgbh/nova/body/extract-your-dna.html

Watch a video to learn how to separate DNA from your cells.

Note: Every effort has been made to ensure that any websites listed above were active at the time of publication. However, because of the nature of the Internet, it is impossible to guarantee that these sites will remain active indefinitely or that their contents will not be altered.

Index